MATERIAL
MATTERS

First published and distributed by
viction:workshop ltd.

viction:ary™

viction:workshop ltd.
Unit C, 7/F, Seabright Plaza, 9-23 Shell Street,
North Point, Hong Kong
Url: www.victionary.com
Email: we@victionary.com
:fb: @victionworkshop
:tw: @victionary_
:ig: @victionworkshop

Edited and produced by viction:ary

Creative direction by Victor Cheung
Book design by viction:workshop ltd.

ISBN 978-988-79033-5-2
Printed and bound in China

MATERIAL
MATTERS

VOLUME
TWO:

METAL

CREATIVE
INTERPRETATIONS
OF
COMMON
MATERIALS

Excerpt by John Heskett

'Design: A Very Short Introduction'
Oxford University Press, 2005

'The human capacity to design has remained constant even though its means and methods have altered, in parallel to technological, organisational, and cultural changes. 'The historical evolution of design' argues that design, although a unique and unchanging skill, has manifested itself in different ways throughout time. The diversity of concepts and practices in modern design is explained by the layered nature of the evolution of design. It is difficult to determine exactly when humans began to change their environment to a significant degree, or in other words to design. Whose interest will design serve in the future? How will design cope with challenges of operating in a more globalised space?"

In what is believed to be his most translated book to-date, writer and educator John Heskett posed some pertinent questions about the future as he perused the application, philosophy, and history of design. Besides underlining the importance of humanising technology and offering readers an exciting glimpse into what could be, Heskett also sought to transform perceptions about design by proving how truly inextricable it is from our daily lives. Instead of merely focusing on the complex inventions that demonstrate how far we have come and how much we are truly capable of achieving for the human race, he examined the simplest of everyday objects to remind us how impactful their designs are and will continue to be, no matter how modest they may seem at first glance.

Fast forward to 2019 where the digital behemoth shows no signs of slowing down since it first appeared, steamrolling over every aspect of our existence. As much as passion and dedication remain timeless humanistic qualities that determine one's progress or trajectory in all fields including art and design, technology has not only broken down physical, spiritual, and ideological barriers, but also opened up whole new dimensions for exploration and experimentation. On a granular level, automation and computerised processes have helped us to do more, get better, and go further than we ever have since the Industrial Revolution in the 18th and 19th centuries; affecting the ways with which we create and appreciate all that is around us.

Although demand plays a big part in determining what gets produced, the market today is often flooded with goods and services that people do not actually need but exist simply because technology and unscrupulous sellers have enabled them to. As consumers become trapped in a mindless cycle of wanting and buying, they end up paying the price in more ways than one - all this because they are being sold ideals and empty messages through advertising and marketing, rather than meaning and purpose. Not all is lost, however, as Heskett's observations are slowly but surely proving to be more relevant than they have ever been.

In recent times, there has been a significant increase in the number of maker communities online and offline, thanks in no small part to the rise in hyper-consumerism and its not-too-distant cousin, the 'throw-away culture'. According to a report by the Royal Society of Arts, the maker movement reflects our society's push against significant technological upheaval, with the underlying goal of giving the power back to the people. Rather than let brands have complete control over our mindsets and habits, what we are saying is 'enough is enough' by choosing self-reliance and a sense of agency. Due to buyers who are becoming more discerning about a product's origins and contents, as well as the craftsmanship and artisanal value behind it, independent sellers are finally seeing their integrity, thoughtfulness, and capabilities be recognised and aptly rewarded.

While this does not mean that mass manufacturing will cease to be a part of our world completely, we are excited about this shift in the realm of art and design. Beyond graphics, illustrations, and colour palettes that are obvious to the naked eye, it is time that materials get the spotlight they deserve. Whether it is used as a textured finish or the canvas of creation itself, the power of material lies in its ability to connect creators to their audiences on a deeper level. Visceral and tactile, it allows every creative experience to evoke an emotional response through touch and feel; universal languages that speak to the senses in a truly authentic manner.

Through our MATERIAL MATTERS series, we hope to inspire readers with the infinite possibilities that embracing, enhancing, and transforming common materials allow for by taking a closer look at the elements that we typically ignore around us. From stamping subtle wood grains onto a piece of stationery to generate a striking pattern to transforming a pristine metal sheet into a rusted sculptural masterpiece, we celebrate the extraordinary beauty in the ordinary, as brought to life across a variety of mediums by the artists and designers featured in our books. After all, just as Heskett posited, means and methodologies of art and design may continue to alter, but at the end of the day, the foundation of creativity as a pure expression of the heart and soul will never falter.

Futuristic-looking yet functional in nature, metal as a material offers numerous conceptual and aesthetical possibilities. Although it may seem inflexible and intimidating at first, it has many attri-butes that can be harnessed to bring complex art and design ideas to life. Malleable and ductile, the characteristics of metal allow for it to be flattened into thin foils and further enhanced with textures to make plain surfaces pop, or stretched into strips and coiled to create distinctive objects that catch the eye. There is even beauty in its decay, as the rust that forms after it is exposed to the elements presents a visceral quality that can evoke different emotions in viewers. Despite the fact that it is recyclable, it is important for us to ensure that metal is used thoughtfully and sustainably so that it can benefit our society for a long time to come.

In featuring as many techniques as possible that bring out its best, all the creative work in this book has been curated based on three key categories that cover the interesting and impactful ways with which the artists and designers have utilised, applied, and pushed the limits of the material.

EMBRACE

Tapping into the inherent physical properties that most metals possess, some artists and designers have realised their creative visions through subtle levels of manipulation to highlight the unique qualities of the material. Whether they have recreated simple metallic forms and effects using technology and the digital medium for artistic purposes or applied metal sheets, sheens, and foils to achieve a sleek and sophisticated aesthetic on their branding work, each featured project is a celebration of metal and its inimitable character.

ENHANCE

Although metal is a relatively strong material, it is possible for artists and designers to leave distinct impressions on them in reflecting their backgrounds, personalities, and styles. Using different techniques such as sandblasting, laser-cutting, or engraving to create new surfaces, textures, and objects, they can find meaningful ways to make their mark and have their messages resonate effectively. From geometric graphics to intricate illustrations, every small detail matters in enhancing the material, as some of the featured work exemplify.

TRANSFORM

Some artists and designers thrive on experimentation, and metal is an interesting material that can be explored to produce a variety of outcomes with. Although its limits can be pushed to a point where its original state is almost unrecognisable, metal has the ability to manifest aspects of its chemical make-up in striking ways to achieve memorable results. Oxidisation, for example, can transform certain metals to look like new matter entirely, and by being as innovative as some of the creatives featured, their potential can truly be limitless.

Plating is a technique that has existed for many years, and continues to play an important part in modern production. It typically involves covering the surface of another material with metal and serves to reduce friction, prevent corrosion, and alter conductivity, among other purposes. In art and design, it is primarily used to decorate objects, such as in giving a shinier finish to jewellery pieces.

There are various methods of plating, but off-the-shelf liquid plating solutions are often utilised for small-scale projects. Besides applying heat and pressure onto a metal sheet to plate, other industrial-style methods also include electro-plating and vapour deposition, where solid metal is vapourised in a vacuum and deposited onto electrically conductive materials.

The type of surface being coated determines the viability of the plating material. In jewellery-making, for instance, gold plating often works for items that will not get heavy wear or friction, like earrings and pendants. Silver plating is generally used to give antique or vintage items a new sheen through 'baths', whereas rhodium plating, which is also known as dipping, is suitable for giving white-gold jewellery a sparkling effect. It is important that a surface is free of dents or scratches and polished thoroughly before plating to achieve the best results.

(Source: en.wikipedia.org)

PLATING

OXIDISING

Oxidation is a process that takes place when a chemical reaction occurs on a metal surface that is exposed to oxygen. It is a form of metal corrosion that changes the surface's colour and texture, resulting in visceral effects that become more obvious over time.

An oxide refers to the combination of oxygen with another element - in this case, metal. Rust is an iron or iron-alloy oxide that can be found within the environment, usually as a result of contact between metal and water or air moisture. Over a prolonged period of exposure, rust can eventually cause the metal mass to disintegrate entirely. Although all the outcomes seem to look alike, different surfaces can rust differently according to the surrounding circumstances. Due to this phenomenon, artists and designers can create various conditions that result in interesting and intriguing outcomes.

studio yumakano strive to explore the unnoticed aspects of everyday. Fascinated by the impact of oxidisation on different materials, their projects on pages 152 to 158 brought together the density of rust and the airy nature of acrylics in the form of rust harvest boxes and furniture. Through this technique, they created compelling organic patterns on what would otherwise be ordinary-looking objects.

(Source: www.thebalance.com)

Laser-cutting was typically used for industrial manufacturing applications in the past due to limited access to technology, but in recent times, the technique has become more accessible to schools, small businesses, and hobbyists alike. It works by directing or focusing a computer-generated laser beam onto a metal surface to cause the melting, burning, or vapourisation of the material.

As laser-cutting does not rely on any physical force, it can separate metals cleanly without creating torn or uneven edges. Metal-cutting machines also allow for more sheet metals to be worked on at the same time; making them suitable for achieving elaborate but precise results in large quantities quickly. Some of these machines can even be used for engraving, another popular technique artists and designers can use to manipulate metal.

Engraving was a historically important method of producing images on paper via copper or steel in artistic printmaking. Today, it is commonplace for retail stores to have graphic design software-equipped computer-controlled engravers to offer personalisation. Unlike industrial ones, retail machines only use one interchangeable 'head' for different finishes, but the possibilities can be truly endless.

(Sources: en.wikipedia.org, www.marlinwire.com)

LASER-CUTTING & ENGRAVING

PAINTING

For many artists and designers, painting is a versatile technique to revamp, rejuvenate, or create one-of-a-kind outcomes by transforming the way a surface looks. Depending on the contents and consistency of the paint, it can even protect a material from the elements. However, not all paint types work on metal surfaces, and using the wrong one can result in unsightliness and damage.

Before painting, it is important to find out what kind of metal is being used, and an easy way to do so is by holding a magnet to it. If the magnet sticks, the metal is most likely ferrous, which means that it contains iron and would be prone to rusting. On the other hand, if the magnet does not stick, it might mean that the metal is galvanised. In both instances, rust, oil, or any leftover paint must be chemically stripped or removed from the surface before the next step.

Once it is clean, a rust-inhibiting oil-based primer should be applied in layers to ensure that paint will adhere well to it. Although acrylic paint is said to work best on metal, the safest way to determine if a paint or primer is suitable is to read the product label and establish that it is formulated as such. Jiyoun Kim Studio™'s project on page 142 exemplifies seamless application of paint on metal. If one is painting on metallic foils, sheets, or smaller surfaces, the entire process can be simplified, as only the right paint needs to be found without having to strip or prime the surfaces.

(Source: www.realsimple.com)

Typically created with malleable metals like aluminium, copper, tin, and gold, foils are very thin metallic sheets that are obtained through hammering or rolling. The more malleable a metal is, the thinner the foil can become. Extremely thin foil is also known as metal leaf, and must be picked up with special tools or brushes as it can tear very easily.

Gold leaf is a popular type of metal leaf that has been used for centuries in art, architecture, and design though gilding: a decorative technique where gold leaf is applied onto solid surfaces made of metal, wood, porcelain, or stone. There is a wide variety of carats and shades available, but the most commonly used leaf is made of 22K yellow gold, as it can be mixed into alloys to add strength and durability.

Many designers use foils to materialise visual identities on stationery and packaging due to their versatile and eye-catching qualities. Although they are delicate to work with, embossing or stamping them with a heat gun or a machine is all it takes to add impact and character to any project.

(Source: en.wikipedia.org)

FOILING

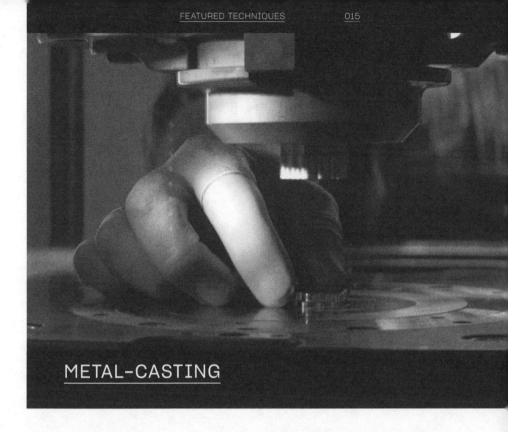

METAL-CASTING

Metal-casting is one of the most common casting processes that has been around for many years. It involves pouring liquid metal into a mould that has a hollow cavity of the desired model or shape, and then allowing the metal to cool and solidify. The solidified part is also known as a casting, which is to be ejected or broken out of the mould with the help of a release agent to obtain the final set result.

Typically, casting creates complex shapes or objects that would be difficult to produce or uneconomical to make by other methods. For certain projects, two moulds are used to constitute two halves of an object, whereas others involve piece-moulding, where a number of different moulds form the shape of a larger and more valuable object when combined. From furniture and household goods to tools, jewellery, and decorative cases,

there are many creative outcomes that can be generated through casting.

London-based Latvian designer Arthur Analts was inspired by Albert Einstein's quote about bees to honour his native country's natural landscape, resources, and sustainability efforts in a meaningful way, as seen on page 84. Basing his concept around the insect to symbolise Latvia's ecological indicator, he casted honeycomb-shaped collector coins in varying frostings, radii, and cell depths to depict the rough outline of Latvia and the Gulf of Riga when put together.

(Source: http://164.100.133.129:81)

WORK TYPE | Packaging
DESIGN | Jens Nilsson
CLIENT | PangPang Brewery

PangPang Brewery, Stock-holm's first microbrewery, is known for its uncon-ventional brewing meth-ods and unique flavours packaged in eye-catching bottle and can designs. For PangPang Can Re-lease, a variety of cloudy canned beer released in bottled form, Jens Nilsson screen-printed die-cut silver foil labels to recreate the aluminium surface of a beer can. An outline of a pull-tab was also printed onto each bottle cap to reinforce the beer's original concept.

PANGPANG CAN RELEASE

PangPang

PANGPANG CAN RELEASE

This cloudy can beer has had enough of seeing its friends cramped up in aluminum containers and sold merely as design items made by over paid digital designs. This beer demand to be seen for the beauty it is. Can Beer is no longer Contained - It must be released!

A CLOUDY CAN BEER RELEASED IN A BOTTLE.

6% ABV · 33 CENTILITER
Mosaic, Citra, Wheat, Oats, Barley.
Innehåller kornmalt. Starköl.

ENTILITER
at, Oats, Barley.
malt. Starköl.

Pang Pang
CAN RELEAS

Pang Pang

beer has
eing its
up in

WORK TYPE | Packaging
DESIGN | Carl Nas Associates
CLIENT | Tangent GC

Specialists in making eco-friendly garment-, shoe-, and skincare products, Tangent GC released a line of organic hand creams that Carl Nas Associates were tasked to design packaging for. Printing the brand's iconic white labels directly onto fully-recyclable glossy aluminium tubes instead of using paper stock, they created an authentic and stylish look for the new range that aptly reflected its underlying ethos.

TANGENT GC
ORGANIC HAND CREAM

TGC205

FIR

hand cream

organic

TANGENTGC

TGC206

TULIP

hand cream

organic

TANGENTGC

TGC206 tulip is a perfumed, organic hand cream - crafted with pure vegetable lipids. Imagine if you will the freshly harvested bouquet: Still cool from outdoors, with close-fitting petals and watery stalks that make a slight squeaking sound when handled. This is our tulip perfume; floral yet cautious. As if it is keeping watch over its promise.

CS Krém na ruce, DA Håndcreme, DE Handcreme, EN Hand cream, ES Crema de Manos, ET Kätekreem, FI Käsivoide, FR Crème mains, IT Crema mani, NL Handcrème, LV Roku krems, NO Håndkrem, PL Krem do rąk, PT Creme para as mãos, SV Handkräm.

Ingredients: Aqua, Glycerin, Sorbitan Olivate, Cetearyl Olivate, Brassica Campestris Seed Oil, Butyrospermum Parkii Butter, Caprylic/Capric Triglyceride, Aloe Barbadensis Leaf Juice, Stearyl Alcohol, Cetyl Alcohol, Cetyl Palmitate, Sorbitan Palmitate, Benzyl Alcohol, Xanthan Gum, Allantoin, Parfum, Salicylic Acid, Sorbic Acid, Citric Acid, Potassium Sorbate, Sodium Benzoate, Limonene, Sodium Sulphite.

Tangent Garment Care AB
Box 4834, 102 61 Stockholm, Sweden
tangentgc.com
Made in Sweden

1.7 fl.oz

e50ml

TGC205

FIR

hand cream

organic

TGC206 tulip is a perfumed, organic hand cream - crafted with pure vegetable lipids. Imagine if you will the freshly harvested bouquet. Still cool from outdoors, with close fitting petals and woody stalks soon after handled. This is our tulip perfume: floral yet courteous. As if it is keeping watch over its promise.

SE Krämena ruce, EN Handcreme, DE Handcreme, ES Crema de Manos, EI Kätevoide, FR Crème mains, IT Crema mani, NL Handcreme, LV Roku krēms, RU Крем для рук, NO Håndkrem, PL Krem do rąk, PT Creme para as mãos, SV Handkräm.

Ingredients: Aqua, Glycerin, Sorbitan Olivate, Cetearyl Olivate, Brassica Campestris Seed Oil, Butyrospermum Parkii Butter, Caprylic/Capric Triglyceride, Aloe Barbadensis Leaf Juice, Stearyl Alcohol, Cetyl Alcohol, Cetyl Palmitate, Sorbitan Palmitate, Benzyl Alcohol, Xanthan Gum, Allantoin, Parfum, Salicylic Acid, Sorbic Acid, Citric Acid, Potassium Sorbate, Sodium Benzoate, Limonene, Sodium Sulphite.

Tangent Garment Care AB
Box 4934, 102 01 Stockholm, Sweden
tangentgc.com
Made in Sweden

1.7 fl.oz

e50ml

TANGENTGC

TGC206

hand cream

TULIP

organic

TGC205

TANGENTGC

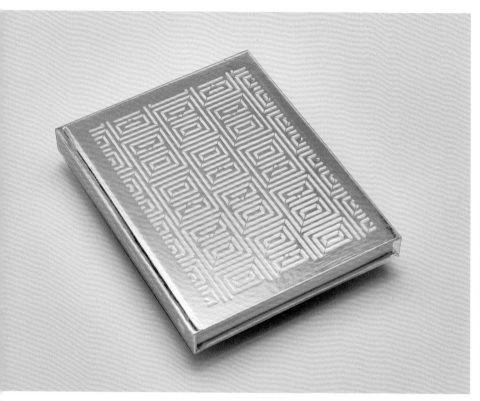

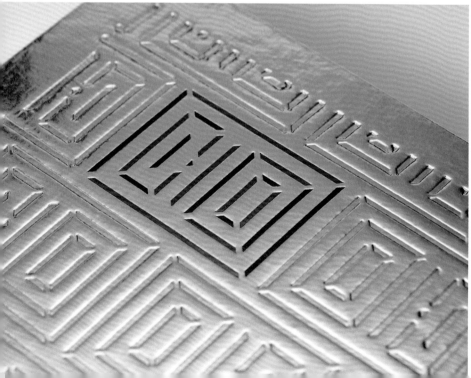

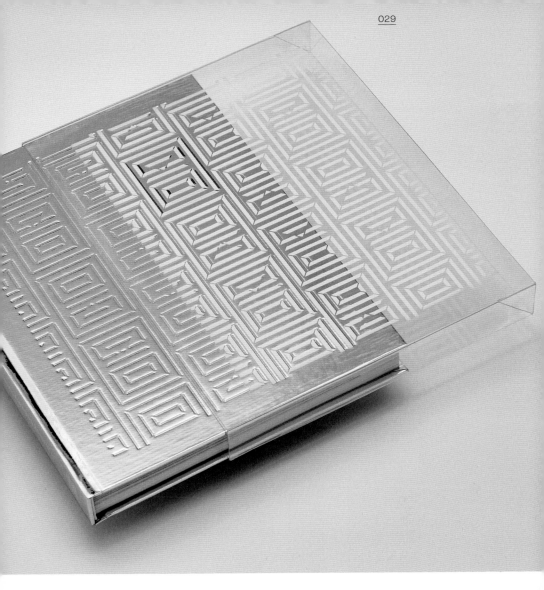

WORK TYPE | Book, Poster

DESIGN | visionplus

CLIENT | The Hong Kong Institute of Architects

The Hong Kong Institute of Architects' annual awards ceremony recognises outstanding works of architecture by its members. For the 2016–2017 edition, visionplus featured a metallic silver sheen throughout their design work to reflect the values of strength and excellence. They also created a key visual element that resembled a brick, which they then 'built' into a geometric pattern on the cover of the event book published for that year.

HKIA ANNUAL AWARDS 2016/17

THE
HONG KONG
INSTITUTE OF
ARCHITECTS
ANNUAL AWARDS
2016/17
FINALISTS
EXHIBITION

香港建築師學會
二零一六/一七年年獎
入圍作品展覽

EXHIBITION PERIOD
25 — 29 October 2017
VENUE
Garden Court, LG1
Pacific Place, 88 Queensway
Hong Kong
Project panels and building models
showcase, creative workshops,
public voting on "My Favourite Building"

覽日期
2017年10月25日至29日

香港金鐘道88號
太古廣場LG1 Garden Court
作品展板及模型展覽、創意工作坊、
公眾投票活動之「我最喜愛建築」

ENRICO CASTELLANI (Castelmassa, 4 agosto 1930 - Celleno, 1° dicembre 2017) è stato un pittore italiano, considerato una delle figure di maggior rilievo dell'arte europea della seconda metà del *Novecento*.

PRINCIPALI ESPOSIZIONI DAL 1999 AL 2017

1999   *GALLERIA LIA RUMMA, MILANO.*
        GALLERIA CIVICA DI ARTE CONTEMPORANEA, TRENTO.

2001   *FONDAZIONE PRADA, MILANO.*

2002   *KETTLE'S YARD, UNIVERSITY OF CAMBRIDGE,*
        CAMBRIDGE (GB).
        GALERIE MEERT RIHOUX, BRUXELLES (B).

2004   *GALERIE DI MEO, PARIGI (F).*

2005   *MUSEO PUSHKIN DELLE BELLE ARTI, MOSCA (R).*

2006   *MÚZEUM MILANO DOBESA, BRATISLAVA (SLK).*
        GALLERIA LIA RUMMA, NAPOLI.
        SPAZIO RISONANZE, AUDITORIUM PARCO DELLA MUSICA, ROMA.

2009   *HAUNCH OF VENISON, NEW YORK (NY, USA).*

2010   *SEOMI GALLERY, SEUL (K).*

2011   *HAUNCH OF VENISON, NEW YORK (NY, USA)*

2012   *GÜNTHER UECKER/ENRICO CASTELLANI - CA' PESARO,*
        GALLERIA NAZIONALE D'ARTE MODERNA, VENEZIA

2013   *GALERÍA CAYÓN, MADRID (ES).*
        GÜNTHER UECKER/ENRICO CASTELLANI, MUSÉE D'ART MODERNE DE
        SAINT-ÉTIENNE, MÉTROPOLE (FR).
        GALLERIA MASSIMO DE CARLO, LONDON (UK).

2014   *LOCAL HISTORY: CASTELLANI, JUDD, STELLA, DOMINIQUE LÉVY GALLERY, NEW*
        YORK (NY, USA) E LONDON (UK)

2015   *ENRICO CASTELLANI E LEE UFAN, LORENZELLI ARTE, MILANO.*

2016   *DOMINIQUE LÉVY GALLERY, LONDON (UK) E NEW YORK (NY, USA).*

2017   *CARL ANDRE E ENRICO CASTELLANI, GALERIE GRETA MEERT, BRUXELLES (B).*

ENRICO CASTELLANI è stato insieme a **Piero Manzoni** e **Agostino Bonalumi**, uno dei grandi animatori dell'arte italiana negli anni sessanta.

IL GRANDE ARTISTA ENRICO CASTELLANI: 1930 - 2017

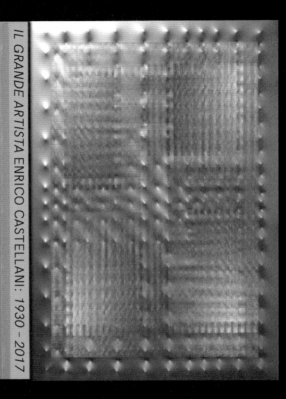

WORK TYPE | Book

DESIGN | Brando Corradini

TYPEFACE | Florian Karsten by Imprint Foundry, Stanley Smith by David Bennewith

Brando Corradini pays tribute to Brâncuși, the patriarch of modern sculpture and one of the most influential sculptors of the 20th century, through the destruction and reconstruction of grids. Combined with the clever use of photography and text, the creative approach for his Constantin Brâncuși editorial project reflects the essence of the artist's own works, which represent the expressions of an authentic pioneer of modernism with hints of Byzantine and Dionysian traditions.

CONSTANTIN BRÂNCUȘI - EDITORIAL

WORK TYPE | Branding, Collateral
DESIGN | Mona Bianca Dürer
3D MODELLING | Georg Gusinski

For PSYCHE. museum, Mona Bianca Dürer developed a compelling visual identity revolving around contorting metals to depict the distortion of perceptions that the mentally ill typically experience. The interaction between the metallic sheens and pill bottle label-like neon strips created a sense of discomfort almost akin to everyday life in psychiatric institutions. Coupled with confrontational headlines, her work set out to help people better understand the patients' plights.

PSYCHE.
PSYCHIATRISCHES
MUSEUM HAINA

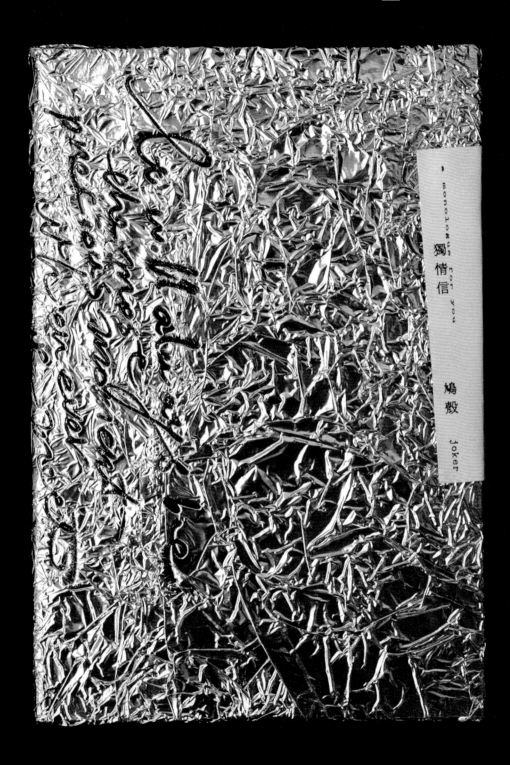

WORK TYPE | Book
DESIGN | mistroom

mistroom published a special 'love letter' comprising 212 poems on the 12th of February, the intended recipient's birthdate. Revolving around a sense of longing and inner conflict, the book's concept was brought to life in the form of a calendar, with each page number representing a date over 212 sequential days. The crushed foil cover served to reflect the impermanence of relationships and how one's crush can often cause turmoil.

A MONOLOGUE FOR YOU

WORK TYPE | Packaging
DESIGN | Futura
PHOTOGRAPHY | Rodrigo Chapa
SPECIAL CREDIT | Mezcal Barro de Cobre

For its ninth anniversary, Futura collaborated with the Barro de Cobre liquor brand to release Revolt is Near, a special-edition twice-distilled mezcal. The underlying concept for its creation was to represent how far the studio had come over the years by challenging old ways, experimenting with new methods, and encouraging chaos. Each label featured a different finish, with the name of the mezcal handstamped on crushed metallic foil to reflect the studio's fearless approach in pushing creative limits.

BARRO DE COBRE

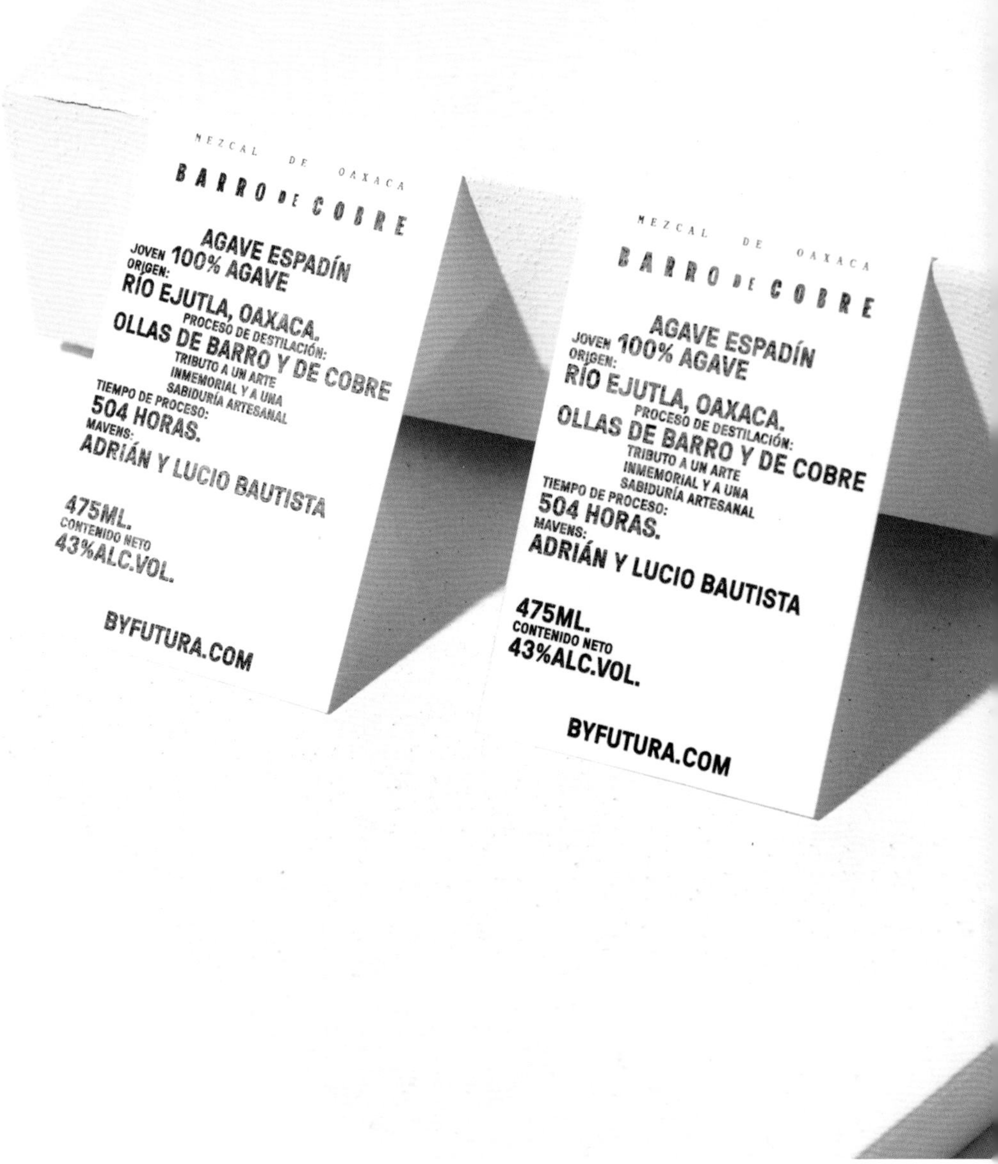

WORK TYPE | Product, Packaging
DESIGN | byHAUS
CLIENT | byHAUS & Monsillage

According to Christian texts, the three wise men who were guided by a star to find the baby Jesus were carrying an offering of gold, myrrh, and incense respectively. Inspired by this classic story, byHAUS designed a nativity-themed gift in the form of a golden bar of soap named Trois Mages. Made of precious balm myrrh and incense, it honoured all those who prefer to give rather than receive, with fitting packaging that featured foil-stamping and deboss-ing printing techniques.

GOLD BAR SOAP

WORK TYPE | Branding, Collateral
DESIGN | vegrande®
CLIENT | Sandra Chuc

Backed by years of experience with a focus on providing high-quality hair styling and make-up services, KEIROS Estilistas is an established beauty parlour in Yucatan. For its rebranding exercise, vegrande® sought to subtly reflect its obsession with excellence by featuring golden vintage elements on a monochromatic base. They also created a special typographic system and custom pattern to embody elegance and an understated sense of luxury.

KEIROS ESTILISTAS

Lealtad.

merece

K Σ I R O S

Queremos demostrarte lo importante
que eres para nosotros.
Sigue disfrutando de nuestro excelente
servicio y recibe beneficios y
experiencias exclusivas

WORK TYPE | Direct Malier
DESIGN | Zone Studio
CLIENT | Le Bon Marché
PHOTOGRAPHY | Younès Klouche
PRINTING | L'Imprimerie du Marais

Le Bon Marché is a high-end departmental store in Paris. To promote the venue to VIPs and luxury hotel dwellers, Zone Studio designed a distinctive direct mailer by transforming its envelope into an eye-catching booklet cover. It featured a golden marquetry pattern created using a 'micro-structure' stamping technique to reinforce the concept of profusion and refinement.

WORK TYPE | Card
DESIGN | Les Graphiquants

To demonstrate the fact that patterns, materials, and printed objects make up a big part of a graphic designer's repertoire, Les Graphiquants created a wish card that featured golden micro-engraving to create a mixture of textures, layers, and depth. Depending on how the card was moved or touched, viewers could obtain different visual outcomes, as the miniscule dots, lines, and waves created playful and surprising effects.

WISH CARD

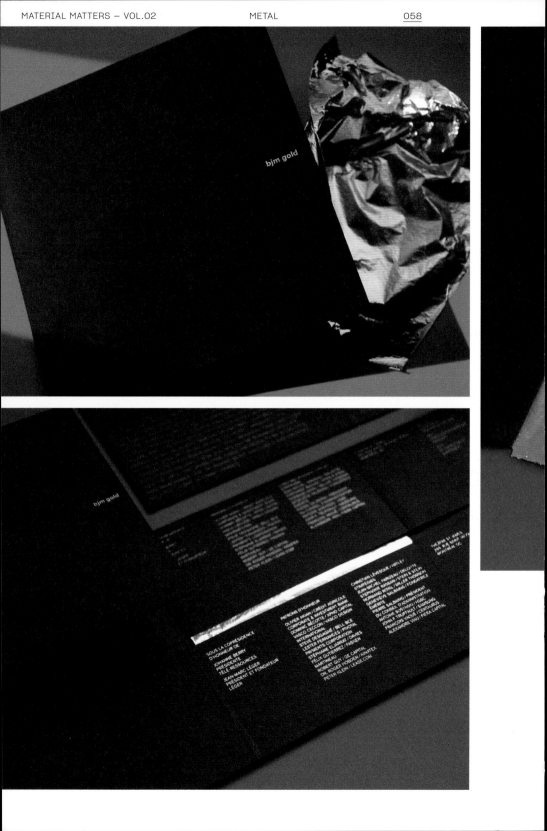

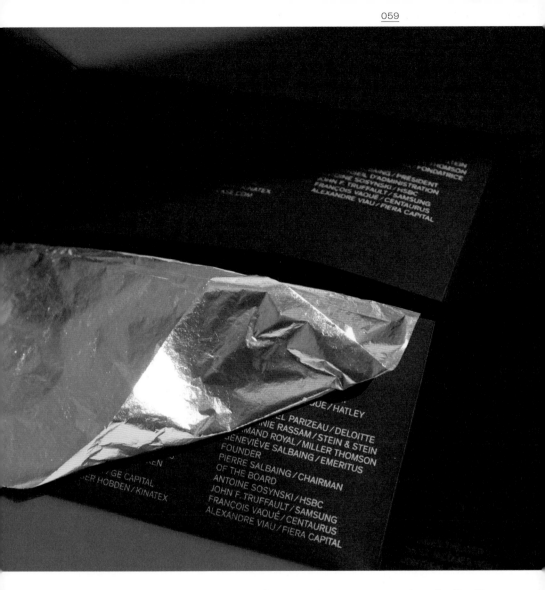

WORK TYPE | Invitation
DESIGN | Paprika
CLIENT | Ballet de Jazz de Montréal (BJM)

Les Ballets Jazz de Montréal is an internationally renowned company that develops unique dance and contemporary ballet performances. For its charity ball at the Théâtre St-James, Paprika were tasked to design invitations that would reflect the event's glamorous nature.

In enhancing its glitzy connotations, the studio used gold leaf sheets with a black base to embody opulence and elegance.

BJM BALLET DE JAZZ DE MONTRÉAL

WORK TYPE | Product, Packaging
DESIGN | Servaire & Co
CLIENT | diptyque paris

Originally patented and designed by Servaire & Co in 2012 to create a dialogue between home scents and time, diptyque's hourglass-shaped diffuser was given an award-winning makeover in 2018. The new edition's unique silhouette and glass coating assert the brand's decorative universe and pay tribute to its eclectic inspirations. Coupled with cold-diffusing technology, each perfume note is delivered through an increased number of wicks for a stronger permeation of fragrance.

DIPTYQUE PARIS -
THE HOURGLASS HOMESCENT
DIFFUSER

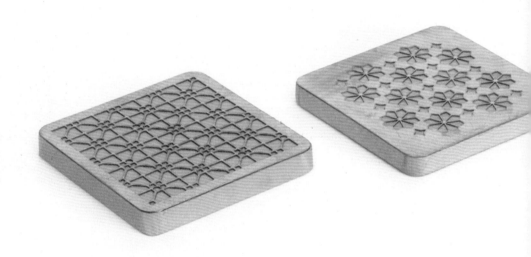

WORK TYPE | Product
DESIGN | okapi studio

In fulfilling its mission to find a balance between urbanisation and the preservation of heritage by celebrating different materials through craftsmanship, okapi studio developed a special series of products comprising bookmarks, coasters, postcards, and incense pots made of galvanised iron and wood. Based on the theme of 'old Hong Kong', they sought to travel through time by deriving visual inspiration from iconic historical elements; fusing creativity and cultural significance to form lasting impressions.

GALVANISED IRON SERIES

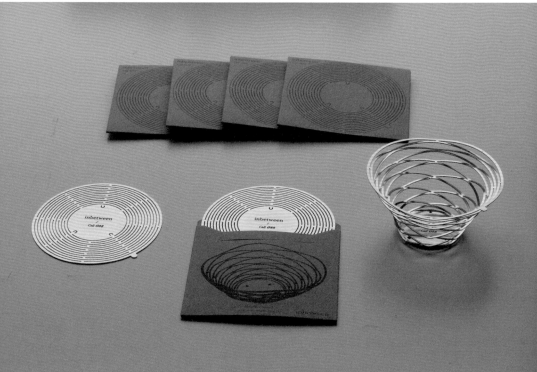

WORK TYPE | Product
DESIGN | studio inbetween

In pushing the boundaries of what a candle holder could be and look like, studio inbetween designed a thoughtful and minimal-ist-chic version using a coil-like brass metal sheet. To use it, one simply need-ed to extend the sheet upwards to give it structure and reveal its distinct aes-thetics. Due to its physical duality and ability to be flat-packed, the candle holder could also be stored or shipped conveniently.

CELL Ø88
BRASS CANDLE HOLDER

WORK TYPE | Event Collateral
DESIGN | IS Creative Studio
CLIENT | Latin American Design

The Latin American Design Festival (LADFEST) in 2016 was a major highlight in Lima's creative events calendar. For its visual identity, IS Creative Studio drew upon the award-winning artists, designers, and studios who were participating that year to make it a gold-standard event. Inspired by hip-hop culture, they used golden chains, medals, stencils, and graffiti to inject a fresh and youthful vibe to the concept of luxury, in that it is recognition gained through hard work.

LADFEST 2016

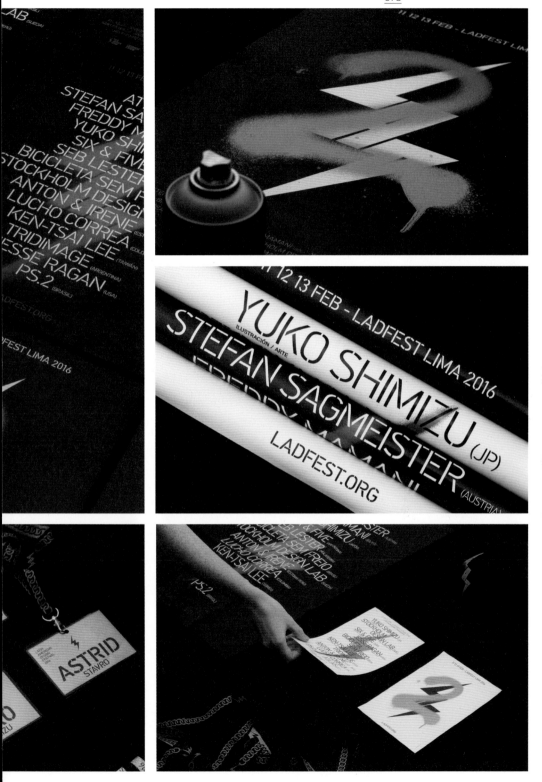

WORK TYPE | Plaque
DESIGN | Duane King

Pioneer 10 was an American space probe that was launched to explore Jupiter and beyond in 1972. Bolted to its antenna support was possibly the most ambitious piece of visual communication ever conceived by NASA at the time: the Pioneer Plaque. Designed by Frank Drake and Carl Sagan with artwork by Linda Salzman Sagan, it served as a cosmic greeting card that would enable mankind to communicate with scientifically educated extraterrestrials. 45 years later, Duane King created a faithful reproduction to celebrate its predecessor's historic journey.

PIONEER –
MESSAGE FROM EARTH

WORK TYPE | Branding, Stationery
DESIGN | Funnel : Eric Kass

In developing his new brand Funnel, Eric Kass sought to create sensorial business cards that would not only leave a memorable impression, but also illustrate his attention to detail, innovation, and quality. Each card featured tiny holes that could funnel light through and formed the constellation for his astrological sign Leo, which the reflective golden sheen also embodied. The cards' irregular shape served to manifest his specialisation in multidimensional packaging design.

FUNNEL :
ERIC KASS IDENTITY

WORK TYPE | Exhibition Collateral
DESIGN | another design
CLIENT | Lianzhou FOTO Organizing Committee
PHOTOGRAPHY | A Rock
TYPOGRAPHY | Zhan Guodong

To lament the replacement of the 'homo faber' with the 'homo consumer' in recent years, the LIANZHOU-FOTO exhibition in 2016 was themed 'As Entertaining As Possible', through which the curator sought to criticise the modern concepts of greed and consumption. In creating its key visual, another design silkscreen-printed gold foil sheets that were subsequently torn and crumpled to illustrate the theme's underlying message of wasteful indulgences.

2016 LIANZHOUFOTO
EXHIBITION IDENTITY

2016 连州国际摄影年展
LIANZHOU FOTO 2016

总监：段煜婷
总策展人：弗朗索·萨瓦尔（法国）／王春辰
策展人：章翔鸥／樊林／沈昭良（台湾）／露西尔·丽博芝（法国）／仲西祐介（日本）／
奥尔加·丝维布洛娃（俄罗斯）／米歇尔·菲利博（法国）
Director: Duan Yuting
Chief Curators: François Cheval (France) / Wang Chunchen
Curators: Zhang Xiangou / Fan Lin / Shen Chao-Liang (Taiwan) / Lucille Reyboz (France) /
Yusuke Nakanishi (Japan) / Olga Sviblova (Russia) / Michel Philippot (France)

无乐不作
As Entertaining
As Possible

11.19-12/09
2016

LIANZHOUFOTO
连州国际摄影年展

总监：段煜婷

总策展人：弗朗索·萨瓦尔（法国）/ 王春辰

策展人：章翔鸥 / 樊林 / 沈昭良（台湾）/ 露西尔·丽博芝（法国）/ 仲西祐介（日本）/
奥尔加·丝维布洛娃（俄罗斯）/ 米歇尔·菲利博（法国）/

Chief Curators: Duan Yuting

Director: Duan Yuting

Chief Curators: François Cheval (France) /

Curators: Zhang Xiangou / Fan Lin / Shen Chao-Liang (Taiwan) / Lucille Reyboz (France) /
Olga Sviblova (Russia) / Michel Philippot (France) /

无乐不作
As Entertaining As Possible

11/19–12/09 2016

LIANZHOUFOTO
连州国际摄影年展

WORK TYPE | Coin

DESIGN | Arthur Analts

CLIENT | Bank of Latvia

PHOTOGRAPHY | Vents Āboltiņš

SPECIAL CREDIT | Issued in 2018 by Bank of Latvia. Struck in 2018 by UAB Lietuvos monetų kalykla (Lithuanian Mint).

Inspired by Albert Einstein's quote, 'if the bee disappeared off the face of the Earth, man would only have four years left to live', Arthur Analts's concept for the 5 Euro collector coin honoured Latvia's sustainability efforts, natural landscape, and resources. His honeycomb design formed a rough geographical outline of the country and the Gulf of Riga, with five capped cells symbolising the coin's face value. As a special touch for collectors, the honeycomb also featured different combinations of frostings, radii, and depths.

5 EURO HONEY COIN

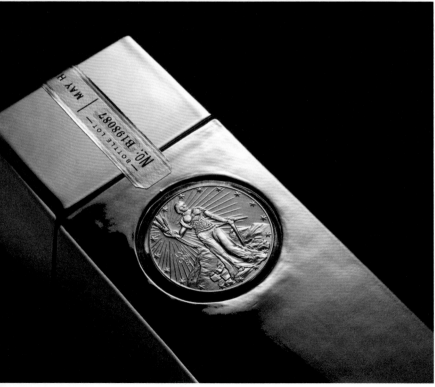

WORK TYPE | Packaging
DESIGN | Chad Michael Studio
CLIENT | Gold Bar Bottle Company

Chad Michael Studio's packaging design for Gold Bar, a luxurious whiskey brand from the Golden State, featured a solid brass coin with every bottle. Besides serving as a symbol of good luck and prosperity, all of the coins were also minted at the oldest private minting company in the US as a subtle nod to the Gold Rush that once took place in California.

GOLD BAR WHISKEY

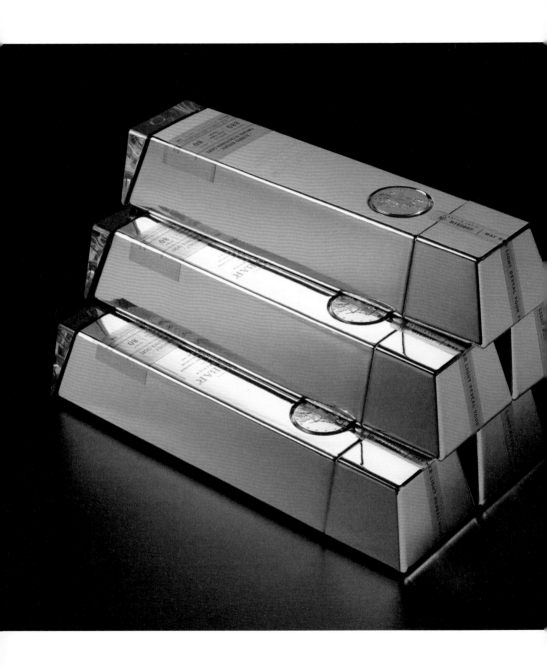

WORK TYPE | Trophy
DESIGN | Studio Wete
CLIENT | IDEP Barcelona
PHOTOGRAPHY | Zoe Difiore, Buen Javier

Every year, IDEP Barcelona awards its best student with the IDEP Gun trophy, which Studio Wete were tasked to create in 2016. In honouring the design school's wishes to use the gun as an analogy for the potentiality of great ideas, they created a special lettering system that inte-grated the names of the trophy and school. They also made the trophy out of metal and spray-painted it with a golden sheen to encapsulate the concept of excellence.

THE IDEP GUN

WORK TYPE | Poster
DESIGN | Studio Blackburn
VISUALISATION | Arteconi CGI

Inspired by the early-20th century Suprematism art movement, Studio Blackburn designed a wall chart for the 2018 World Cup matches in Russia depicting a deconstructed football pitch with bold Russian typography. Through simple geometric shapes and a limited colour palette, they sought to offer fans a visually appealing alternative to the garish and unattractive wall charts typically displayed in public spaces during global tournaments.

WORLD CUP WALL CHART

WORK TYPE | Branding, Stationery
DESIGN | Monotypo Studio
CLIENT | MAXICO Travel Agency
PHOTOGRAPHY | Diana Cristina Espinoza

Mexico is known for being rich in traditional arts and culture. Inspired by this, Monotypo Studio drew upon Huichol handicrafts and tapestry patterns to create a meaningful visual identity for Maxico, a travel agency specialising in trips to local Magical Villages. In complementing its namesake that combines the words 'magic' and 'Mexico', they designed a logo featuring the eagle, an iconic animal in pre-Columbian culture, to symbolise the four cardinal points that tourists could set off on memorable journeys from.

MAXICO

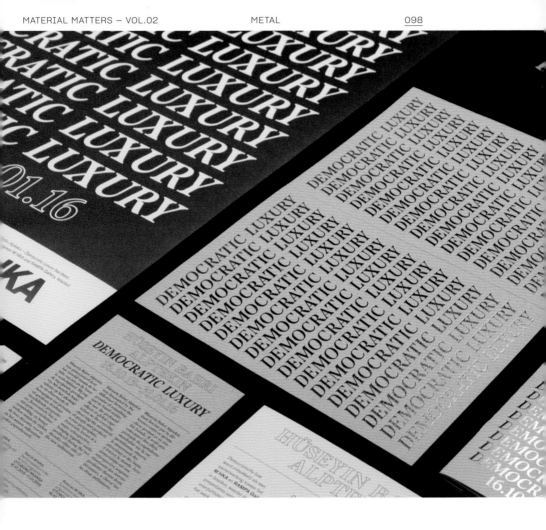

WORK TYPE | Exhibition Collateral
DESIGN | Jelle Maréchal
CLIENT | M HKA - Museum of Contemporary
Art Antwerp

Hüseyin Bahri Alptekin was fascinated by the differences between a promise and the eventual revelation of its banal reality. For the artist's exhibition themed 'Democratic Luxury', Jelle Maréchal developed a simple graphic system that reflected the former's ideas. The designer contrasted high-end luxury materials like gold with basic materials like cardboard and graphic conventions generally associated with mass consumption to juxtapose expectations with actuality.

HÜSEYIN BAHRI ALPTEKIN: DEMOCRATIC LUXURY

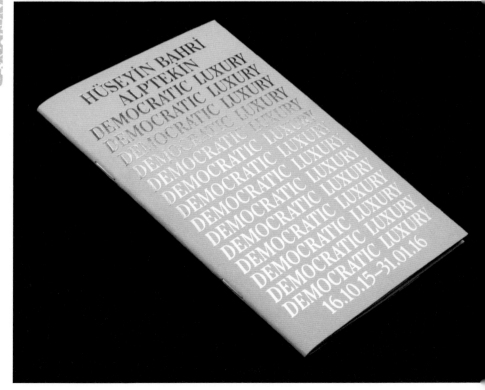

Rotation
typography

WORK TYPE | Type

DESIGN | Txaber Mentxaka

As a typographic experiment, Txaber Mentxaka manipulated metallic 3D blocks to create statement-making letters. By rotating parts of each alphabet's geometry, he produced a strong yet recognisable set of sculptures that were full of character and further enhanced by a sense of movement. The brass finish served to add a sense of authenticity and subtle sophistication.

ROTATION TYPOGRAPHY

Rotation typography. © Txaber 2018

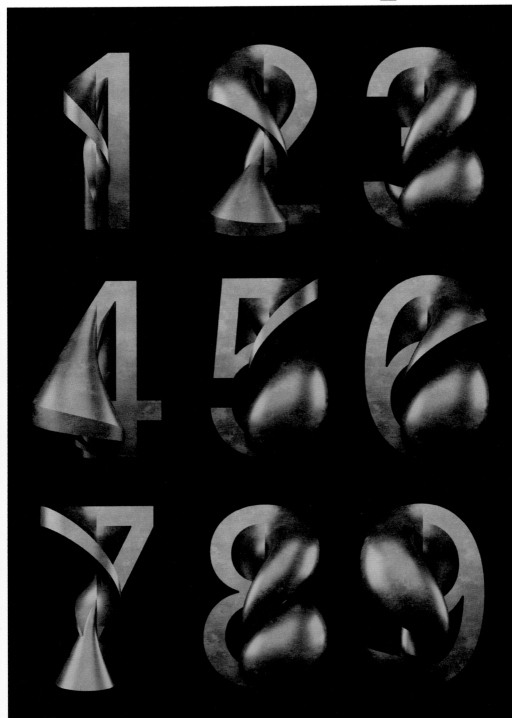

Rotation typography. © Txaber 2018

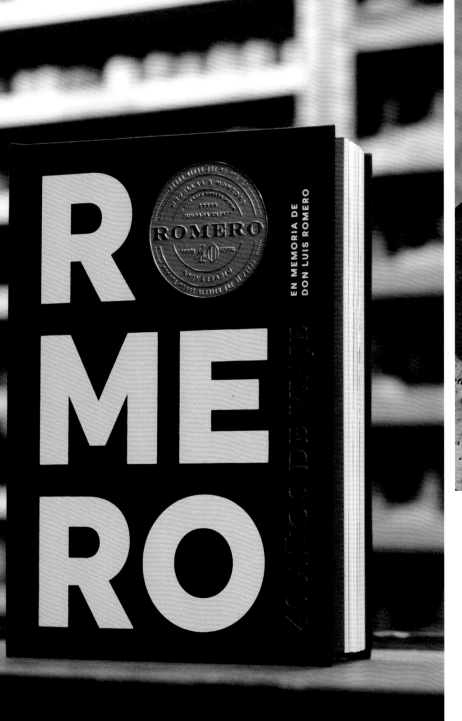

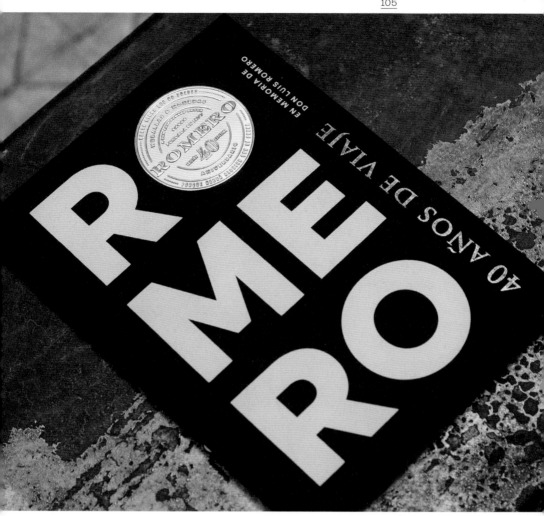

WORK TYPE | Book
DESIGN | Cocoa Branding
CLIENT | Medallas y Monedas Romero
PHOTOGRAPHY | Gilberto Torres
COPYWRITING | Idalia López
PRINTING | Impronta Casa Editora

ROMERO, MEDALS & COINS:
40TH ANNIVERSARY
COMMEMORATIVE BOOK

Cocoa Branding were commissioned by Medallas y Monedas Romero to design a meaningful gift for Jesús Romero Sr., the company's co-founder and CEO. To celebrate his contributions and extraordinary legacy, his children and closest colleagues were tasked to secretly compile personal stories and photographs of him spanning his career. All of their contributions were collated and published as a commemorative book with a specially-minted coin that was gifted to him during the company's 40th anniversary ceremony.

NAVEGA, VELERO MÍO, SIN TEMOR, QUE NI ENEMIGO NAVÍO NI TORMENTA, NI BONANZA TU RUMBO A TORCER ALCANZA, NI A SUJETAR TU VALOR.

José de Espronceda

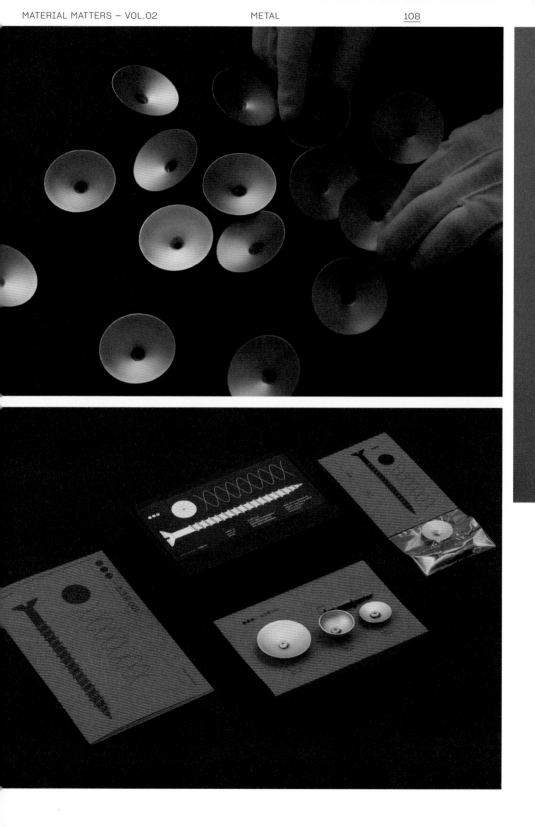

WORK TYPE | Product
DESIGN | BKID
PHOTOGRAPHY | Kim Kwon-jin Studio

In creating their latest product, BKID derived inspiration from a screw's original function, as well as the fact that it is usually hidden in construction. Although screws are not regarded as mere 'asterisks' or extra components in the assembly process, their form does not tend to reflect how important they are, or how they are also subjected to the strictest quality standards. Screw 001 was an innovative manifestation of what screws could look like to transform product design and production processes in the future.

WASHER001

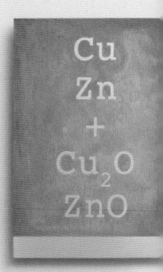

WORK TYPE | Art
ARTWORK | Lex Pott
CLIENT | Found by James

In a bid to draw attention to the contrasts between natural and industrial creations, Lex Pott displayed common metals such as brass, aluminium, and copper in their processed and oxidised states for his True Colours project. Inspired to depict the true meaning of colour, he experimented by exposing their metal coatings to oxygen, moisture, and atmospheric gasses to form various patina outcomes. Depending on the type of metal used, patina has the ability to reveal practical information about the material's origins.

TRUE COLOURS MINIATURES

Al
+
Al_2O_3

Cu
Zn
+
CuO
ZnO

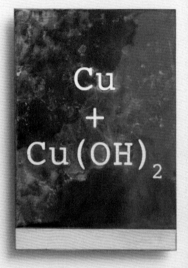

Cu
+
$Cu(OH)_2$

WORK TYPE | Invitation
DESIGN | Boom Creative
CLIENT | Fyodor Golan
PHOTOGRAPHY | Tom Bird

FyodorGolan is a contemporary brand that combines the ease of luxury sportswear with thoughtful, elevated aesthetics. For their AW17 London Fashion Week show themed 'Never Just A Little', Boom Creative were approached to design invitations that would complement the bold, vibrant, and futuristic collection being shown. They mounted fluorescent Gmund Action stock onto a plain fluted board and hand–sprayed the invites with MTN 94 paint to achieve striking results. A blind embossing effect was then applied using clear matt foil for further visual impact.

FYODOR GOLAN: NEVER JUST A LITTLE

WORK TYPE | Packaging
DESIGN | Backbone Branding
CLIENT | Messier 53 Hotel Yerevan
ARCHITECTURE | Hayk Voskanyan

Named after a French astronomer who was the first to compile a catalogue of astronomical objects, Messier 53 is a boutique hotel that embodies the spirit of discovery by taking its guests on a 'mystical journey through the universe'. Deriving inspiration from its strong underlying concept, visual identity, and architecture, Backbone Branding's packaging design for the hotel's guest kits and amenities revolved around structure and space, with each item depicting a distinct mood.

MESSIER 53
HOTEL YEREVAN

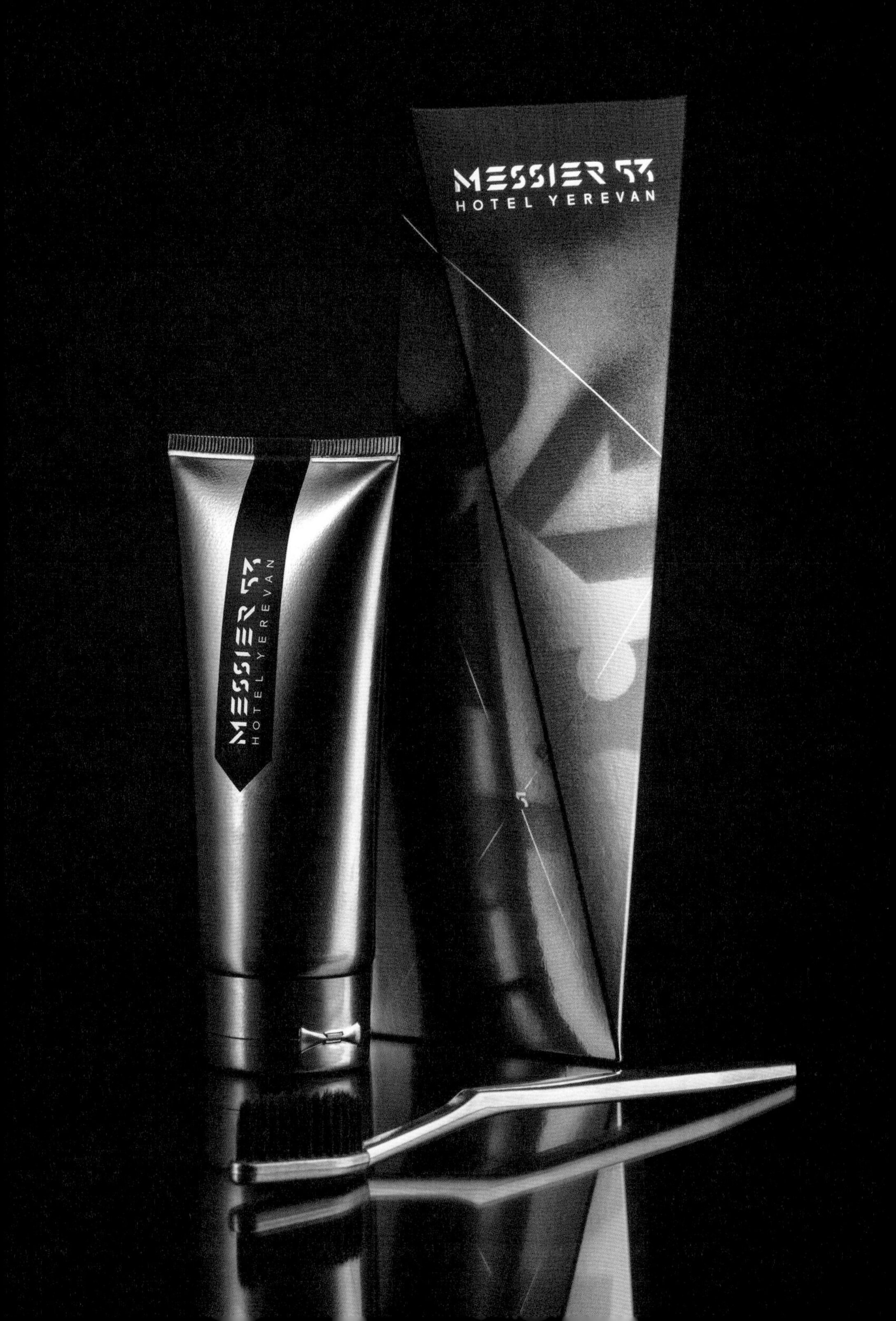
MESSIER 53
HOTEL YEREVAN
MESSIER 53
HOTEL YEREVAN

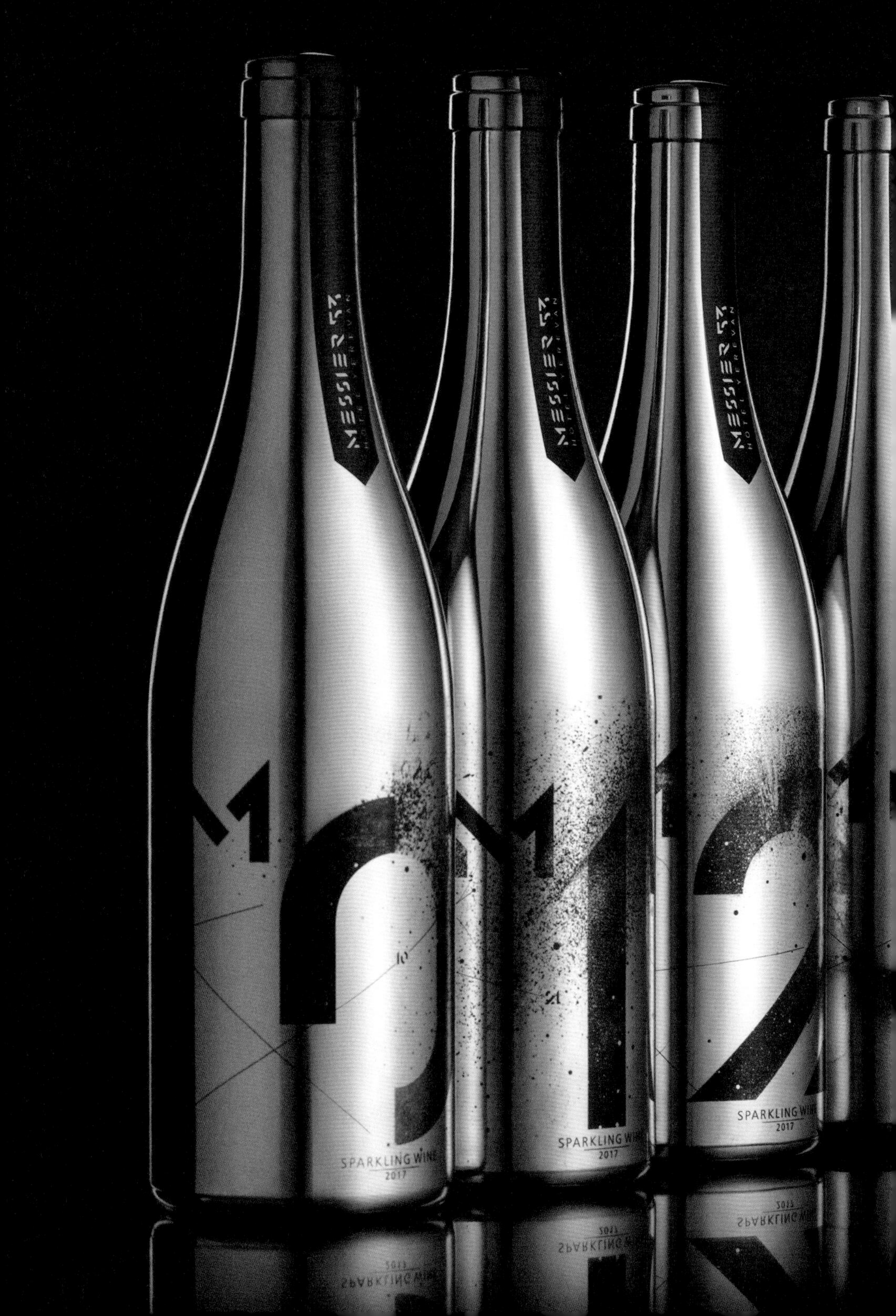
MESSIER 57
HOTEL YEREVAN
SPARKLING WINE
2017

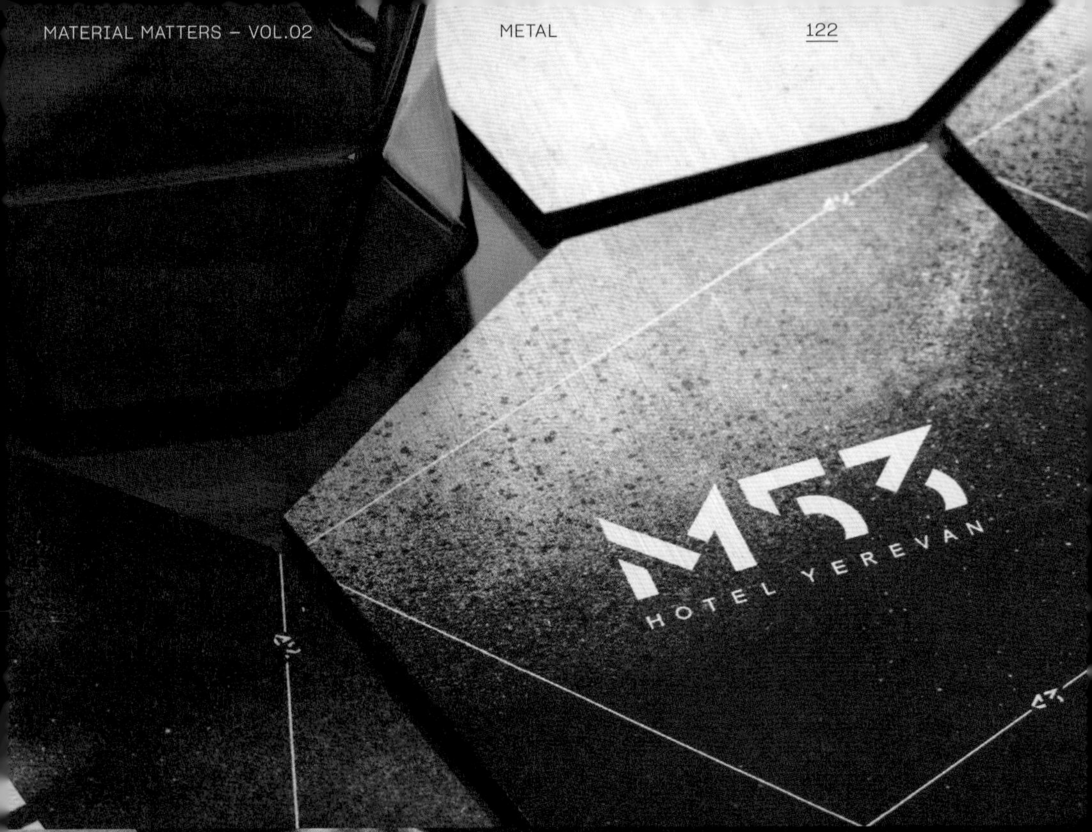

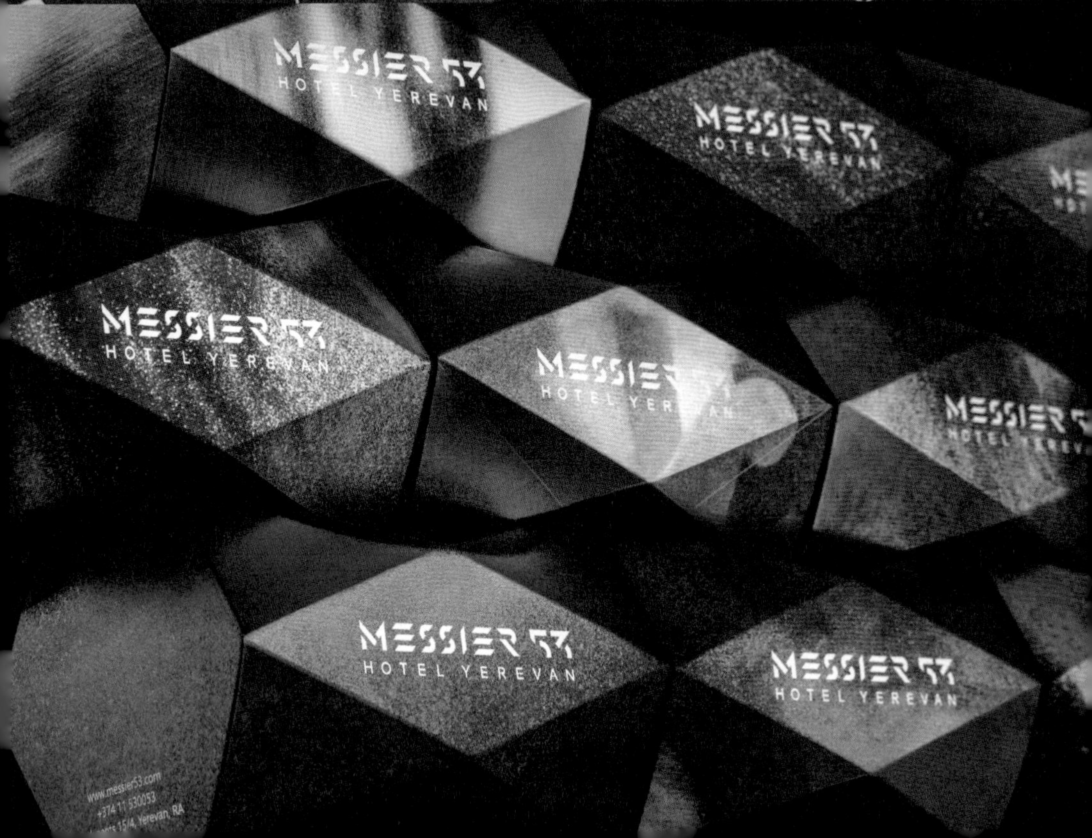

WORK TYPE | Product
DESIGN | Tom Dixon

From the rawness of cast metals to the aesthetical possibilities of vacuum-metallised plastics, materiality is an underlying theme in all of Tom Dixon's work. The Materialism series consists of innovative scents with expertly hand-picked notes that were combined to create an evocative sensorial experience. Each wax and diffuser container is made of honest materials ranging from raw cork and marble to 100%-cast aluminium and iridescent glass for added tactile dimension.

MATERIALISM- OIL

WORK TYPE | Product
DESIGN | Candice Blanc & Ulysse Martel
CLIENT | Nov Gallery
PHOTOGRAPHY | Raphaëlle Mueller

In the near future, humankind's progress in genetics and bio-technology will render physical workouts and efforts to reach physical perfection superfluous. With this concept in mind, Candice Blanc and Ulysse Martel created the Olympia collection comprising a trio of free weights, a pair of push-up bars, and a two-hand dumbbell. Made of steel with a lacquered finish, their architectural aesthetics doubled their functionalities as exercise equipment and decorative sculptures for the home.

OLYMPIA

WORK TYPE | Packaging
DESIGN | Ideando
CLIENT | Xi Ming Cha Ye
COLLABORATION | Yi Xiang Advertising

Inspired by the thickness of Niukui Tea, Ideando set out to reflect the impact of its robust taste through a packaging design concept not commonly associated with tea brands. A simple yet solid colour palette of black and brass was used; drawing focus to the logo cubes embedded into the outerside of the lacquer-ware, as well as the embossed logotype on the tea container within. Coupled with a monochromatic label detailing the ingredients in classic type, the outcome balanced strength and sophistication.

NIUKUI TEA

WORK TYPE | Direct Mailer
DESIGN | Sagmeister & Walsh
CLIENT | Two Trees Real Estate

Sagmeister & Walsh were tasked by Two Trees Real Estate to design a mailer for CEOs who might be interested in moving their companies to the latter's Domino Sugar Factory property. To instantly capture these typically time-starved CEOs' attentions, they laser-cut each recipient's face onto a bronze slip cover. For the information booklet, they designed custom photo-illustrations using only sugar and sugar cubes to depict relevant statistics about the property and its immediate neighbourhood.

DOMINO SUGAR FACTORY

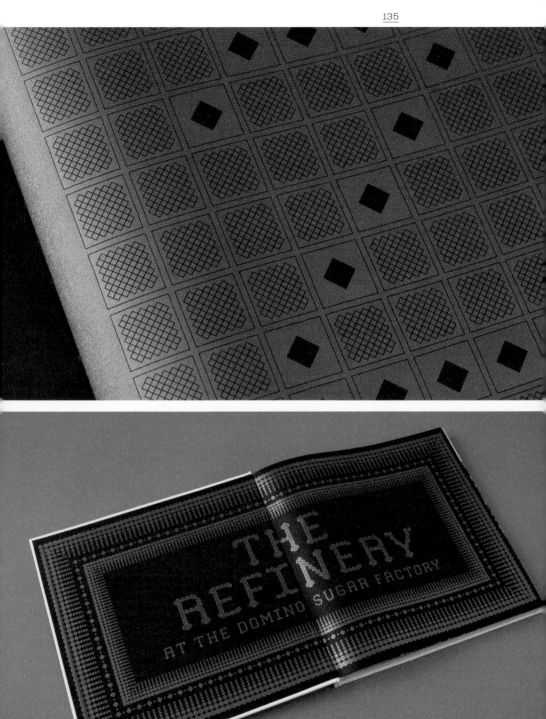

WORK TYPE | Branding, Stationery
DESIGN | MIUNA
CLIENT | Lázaro Casas - Photography Studio
PHOTOGRAPHY | Chino Zenteno

Photography is a powerful means to treasure special moments, particularly for pregnant women, brides, and mothers at Mexican quinceañeras. In turning the Lázaro Casas logo into a full-fledged branding suite for the photography studio, MIUNA revolved their creative concept around this universal insight and its corresponding qualities such as preciousness. Understanding the importance of reliving memories, their design work also featured colours and graphic elements full of nostalgic charm.

LÁZARO CASAS
PHOTOGRAPHY STUDIO

WORK TYPE | Branding, Stationery

DESIGN | Patryk Hardziej

CLIENT | MOTIV STUDIO

MOTIV is an architecture and visualisation studio that focuses on innovative approaches through cutting-edge technology. In a comprehensive rebranding exercise to illustrate its specialisations more effectively, Hardziej Studio designed a flexible visual identity where sim-

ple bronze lines could be combined in clever ways to form complex shapes; cementing MOTIV's position among the leaders in the 3D visualisation industry.

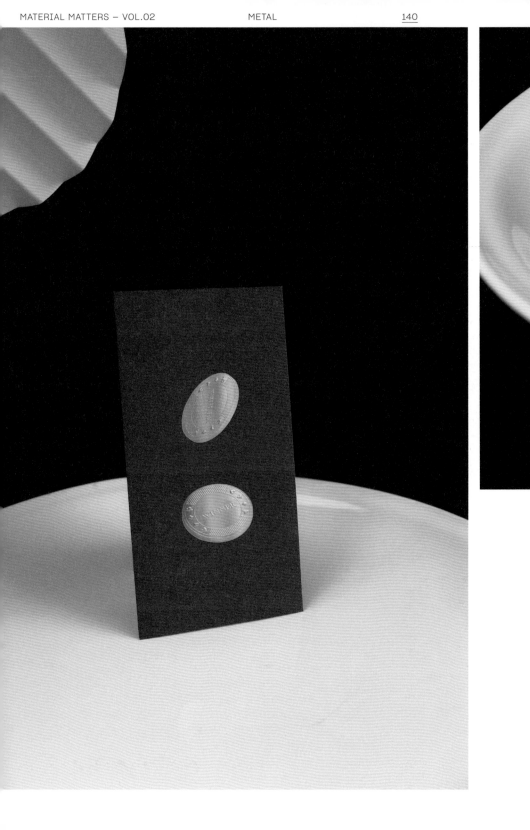

WORK TYPE | Product
DESIGN | (shame-on-you) office
3D FOIL STAMPING | SENSIN Production

FOOLPROOF is a series of products that set up an infallible system for life. Its red pocket sets feature three special visual elements that represent the conquering of various stages in a typical Chinese wedding 'door game'. For the first stage of 'opening the door', the one with the Electric Blue Key design can be used, followed by the one with the Shiny Silver Bank Card design to 'bribe the bridesmaids'. At last, to celebrate 'reaching the bride', the one with the Lavish Gold Coins design can be distributed.

FOOLPROOF RED POCKET SET

WORK TYPE | Art
ARTWORK | Jiyoun Kim Studio™
CLIENT | Seoul Government

Hangang Art Park is an initiative that was launched by the Seoul government to introduce and inject art into the public parks by the Han river. Based on the theme 'Suim' which translates to 'rest' in English, Jiyoun Kim created stools that were inspired by the Dokkaebi, an imaginary monster frequently mentioned in old Korean folklore. Unlike the scary trolls featured in many Western tales, the Dokkaebi have a joyful spirit that rewards people for their good deeds.

DOKKAEBI STOOL

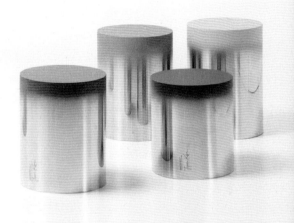

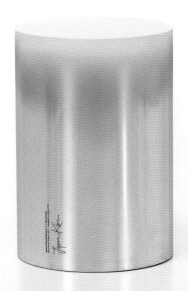

WORK TYPE | Branding, Stationery
DESIGN | Overdrive Design
CLIENT | Heather + Little

Heather + Little has been a leader in custom ornamental and historic sheet metal restorations since 1925. To encapsulate the company's craftsmanship, innovative spirit, and attention to detail in a distinctive way, Overdrive Design created a visual identity that utilised every element, space, and stroke in its logo. Influenced by the Arts and Crafts movement as well as the characteristics of copper, Heather + Little's main working material, they used verdigris or weathered copper to depict beauty and longevity.

HEATHER + LITTLE

WORK TYPE | Packaging
DESIGN | KOREFE
CLIENT | Weingut Knipser

Knipser has been producing high-quality red wines since the early 1980s from its base in Pfalz. For its Knipser 2012 CUVéE XR special-edition wine, KOREFE developed exclusive copper jackets that could visually depict the drink's maturing process. Based on the winery's belief that 'true greatness comes with age', their minimalistic yet meaningfully crafted design served to demonstrate the wine's distinct character through the changing surface colours and haptics.

AGEING WINE BOTTLES

WORK TYPE | Art
ARTWORK | studio yumakano
PHOTOGRAPHY | Satoru Ikegami

studio yumakano created Rust Harvest Boxes by using the outcomes of a rust-gathering project. Appearing at first glance to be brick-like objects, the boxes came into being when their lids were removed and items were placed inside them; revealing their translucent qualities. By bringing together the density of rust and the airy nature of acrylics, the studio created various patterns that pushed the possibilities of natural processes, creativity, and functionality.

RUST HARVEST BOX

WORK TYPE | Product
DESIGN | studio yumakano
PHOTOGRAPHY | Satoru Ikegami

In extending the possibilities of their rust-harvesting exercise, studio yumakano created stylish furniture pieces such as shelves and cupboards from the speckled acrylic tiles. Setting out to disprove the fact that rust is merely an age-old problem in manufacturing by studying it in-depth and creating unique yet functional products out of the colourful results obtained from controlling rust outbreaks, they celebrated the extraordinary beauty in the ordinary.

RUST HARVEST FURNITURE

THE
MATERIAL
-

METAL *(n.)*

UK & US / ˈmet.əl/

[countable or uncountable]

a chemical element, such as iron or gold, or a mixture of such elements, such as steel, that is generally hard and strong, and through which electricity and heat can travel

TYPES

'Metal' is a broad term that spans heavy metals like lead, lightweight metals like aluminium, and liquid metals like mercury at room temperature. Generally, metals are categorised according to their physical or chemical properties. As such, the same metal can sometimes fall under several different classifications.

FERROUS METALS

Ferrous metals include any combinations of metal that contain iron. They are very hardy and often used to make heavy machinery or equipment. Although they can withstand harsh environmental conditions, they corrode over time. Examples: Iron, steel

NON-FERROUS METALS

Non-ferrous metals are used in place of iron to make machinery or equipment. Although they are not as hardy as ferrous metals, they are less corrosive and need less pressure to be moulded into any form. Examples: Aluminium, copper

NOBLE / PRECIOUS METALS

Noble/precious metals can easily be moulded into different forms. As they are highly malleable and do not corrode or rust upon exposure to air, they are expensive and commonly used to make jewellery or coins. Examples: Gold, platinum, silver

HEAVY METALS

Heavy metals are not commonly used due to their high atomic weight and density. Although some of them are easily obtainable, they are also often weaker than more common metals or poisonous when ingested. Examples: Arsenic, cadmium

METAL ALLOYS

Metal alloys are made of a combination of metals to customise desirable attributes like greater strength, durability, and resistance to corrosion. They can also be used to avoid or resist heat generation. Examples: Steel, brass, bronze

STRUCTURE

The key characteristics of metal such as its magnetic properties and ability to conduct electricity and heat hint at its unique internal structure. Due to an 'agile' make-up that contributes to its distinct attributes, metal forms the foundation of many modern creations that are fundamental to the development of societies.

DELOCALISED ELECTRONS

Metals are composed of atoms held together by strong bonds in an orderly pattern. All atoms have electrons on their outer shell, but the electrons on metal atoms are delocalised or free to move; resulting in their strong yet malleable nature, as well as their magnetism and conductivity.

ORES

Generally, metals do not occur in nature the way we need them to, namely in their pure form and in large-enough quantities. They are often buried with deposits of other metals, rocks, and naturally occurring solid compounds known as ores.

PURE METALS

To produce large-enough quantities of the common metals we use such as iron, aluminium, or copper in their pure form, ores need to be extracted from a mine or quarry and then refined. This involves a mixture of mechanical processing, as well as chemical and electrical treatments.

KEY PROPERTIES

DENSE

Solid metals will typically sink when submerged in water at room temperature - the latter depending on size or weight. They are also crystalline in nature, which means that their atoms are arranged in a highly ordered microscopic structure.

DUCTILE

Due to their atomic structure, most metals are malleable. Although they can be bent, hammered, and drawn out into wires or threads without breaking, repeated stresses or 'stretching' can cause them to eventually snap as their atomic bonds weaken.

CONDUCTIVE

Most metals are good electrical and thermal conductors because their delocalised electrons allow electric currents and heat to flow through them easily. However, at room temperature, they are cold to the touch because they also disperse heat quickly.

MAGNETIC

Not all metals are magnetic. However, those that are, such as iron, nickel, cobalt, and the metal alloys that contain them, have the ability to power some of the best magnets in the world.

SUSTAINABILITY

Due to their close links to economic growth, technological advancement, and our well-being as a whole, the demand for metals has grown rapidly over the last few centuries and shows no signs of slowing down. As a consequence, most of the world's metal stocks are being mined and utilised today, instead of remaining as unused reserves.

Fortunately, metals are inherently recyclable, which means that in principle, they can be used and re-used to minimise negative environmental impact and save energy in the long run. However, metal recycling is generally low on the global scale and has yet to be prioritised. As many modern devices contain rare and critical metals, it is imperative that we begin increasing our sustainability efforts to ensure that this valuable resource remains available for future use.

All dictionary definitions are from dictionary.cambridge.org.
All information is correct as of 2019 from www.explainthatstuff.com,
en.wikipedia.org, and studyread.com. Please visit the websites for
more information and links to further resources.

another design

another design is a transmedia visual design team in Guangzhou whose members specialise in graphic design, multimedia design, product design, and photography. It seeks to challenge traditional ways of thinking, expand the boundaries of the design language, and explore the diversity of design in different fields. Based on strategies that cross cultures and businesses, the multidisciplinary yet integrated team provides professional services and innovative strategies that balance cultural and commercial impact.

Arthur Analts

Arthur Analts is a London-based Latvian artist and designer. His work takes a critical look at political, cultural, and environmental issues using a research-led approach with innovative experimentation across materials, new technologies, alternative production techniques, and scale. Although he works with various media, Arthur's methodology is consistent, in that the subject matter of each project determines the material and form it takes; and the outcome is always emotionally charged.

Backbone Branding

Backbone Branding is an independent branding studio in Yerevan that functions as a creative business partner to clients who are ready for extraordinary solutions. To deliver effective results, it digs deep into a brand's essence to understand its values and ingrain them into the design process for relevant and engaging outcomes.

BKID

Adopting a human-centric design-based approach by analysing user needs, behaviours, and desires, BKID is an award-winning studio in Seoul. Set up by Bongkyu Song, it works with various local and international clients to increase brand value and sales results.

Boom Creative

Boom Creative is a UK-based creative direction and graphic design practice that works across a diverse range of platforms and disciplines.

Brando Corradini

Brando Corradini is a graphic designer in Rome who focuses on brand identity, illustration, editorial design, typography, lettering, and digital art. His work life is a direct manifestation of his childhood passions for drawing, graphics, and art, which continue to grow today through various personal and professional projects. A graduate of the Academy of Fine Arts in Rome (RUFA), Brando currently collaborates with the We Meet Brands creative agency.

byHAUS

byHAUS is the design studio of Philippe Archontakis and Martin Laliberté, two accredited graphic designers based in Montreal who specialise in creating distinctive identities that drive success.

Candice Blanc & Ulysse Martel

Architect Candice Blanc and product design-er Ulysse Martel set out to initiate dialogues, challenge their achievements, and create new learning paths in their creative fields through their collaboration. The Future Artefacts project presented the duo with the perfect opportunity to express themselves on their particular themes of interest, such as space, innovation, sport, and antiquity.

Carl Nas Associates

Carl Nas Associates is a London-based design consultancy that operates on the basis that 80 percent of all sensory impressions are visual. It believes that design is a global language that can communicate what needs to be said in an instant, and when done well, can be bespoke and impossible to copy.

Chad Michael Studio

Focusing exclusively on packaging design for alcohol, tobacco, and cannabis brands, Chad Michael Studio is a niché design company in Texas that believes strongly in the power of a direct client-and-designer relationship; in that the best results are often produced when the designer is as passionate about the project as the client.

Cocoa Branding

Cocoa Branding strives to tell a compelling story for every project. The Guadalajara-based studio believes that a brand with a solid con-cept does not need any explanation, as all the visual elements will come together to form a subtle yet powerful singular narrative.

Duane King

Duane King is a consultant and creative direc-tor with a passion for the aesthetics of ideas. Working across mediums from his base in Portland, he co-ordinates relationships among people and concepts to create compelling outcomes and inform the shape of culture. Du-ane is also an executive member of the IADAS and one of Fast Company's 50 Most Influential Designers in America.

Funnel : Eric Kass

Funnel is Eric Kass's fine commercial art prac-tice, where he puts his head, heart, and hands to work in crafting bespoke design solutions for a wide range of clients spanning Hollywood stars and Fortune 500 companies. His skills were honed by over 25 years of diverse design experience collaborating with a variety of arti-sanal, boutique, and emerging brands.

Futura

Futura was founded in 2008 by Vicky González and Iván García. The intersection of two differ-ent backgrounds and working methods gave the Mexico City-based studio a unique way of approaching projects and finding the balance between stiffness and rebellion. As experts in branding, its scope goes beyond visuals to add value to its clients' businesses.

Ideando

Ideando, which was rebranded to 7654321 Studio, is a Fuzhou-based design office that integrates innovation and execution. It provides design and consulting services for clients in the commercial and cultural sectors by understanding contexts, defining concepts, striving for accuracy and clarity, as well as building relationships and experiences.

IS Creative Studio

Pages 070-073

IS Creative Studio specialises in differentiating, observing, and analysing trends to create new benchmarks and successful strategies. With offices in Lima and Madrid, the team uses its global vision, intuition, and sensitivity to transform perceptions, maximise value propositions, and revolutionise brand experiences.

Jelle Maréchal

Pages 098-099

Originally from Antwerp and currently based in Toronto, Jelle Maréchal is a designer and art director who creates meaningful solutions in visual identity, environments, and editorial projects for commercial and cultural clients. As the current associate creative director at Bruce Mau Design, he has worked with many notable clients and brands across the world.

Jens Nilsson

Pages 018-023

Jens Nilsson is a Stockholm-based award-winning graphic designer, art director, and all-round great guy with over 10 years of industry experience. He is also a former art director at the notorious design agency, Snask, and a 2004 Hyper Island alumnus.

Jiyoun Kim Studio™

Pages 013, 142-147

Jiyoun Kim Studio™ is a design consulting agency in Seoul that was founded in 2009. The team's creative approach revolves around communication-based design; a methodology that chief designer Jiyoun Kim developed based on his experiences in the manufacturing and advertising industries. It currently works on a variety of branding, product, furniture, spatial consulting and art projects.

KOREFE

Pages 150-151

KOREFE is the product innovation, visual development, and digital design arm of Kolle Rebbe, a creative agency in Germany that focuses on creative business intelligence and invests in good ideas to support start-ups and founders. It explores new ways for brands to communicate and interact with their customers by unifying the diverse experiences and multidisciplinary skills of the team.

Les Graphiquants

Pages 056-057

Founded in Paris in 2008, Les Graphiquants is a design agency that transforms clients' stories into unique outcomes without losing meaning or its inimitable sense of peculiarity. Its experimental approach always combines intelligence and imagination through rigorous work methods that manifest themselves through typography, branding, art direction, signage, graphic as well as web design projects.

Lex Pott

Pages 112-115

Rotterdam-based experimental designer Lex Pott employs a raw and intuitive method in his work by returning to the origins of the materials he uses most: wood, stone, and metal. A graduate of the Design Academy Eindhoven, he does not hide his designs under indirect layers.

mistroom

Pages 038-039

Founded in 2010 by Taiwan-based designers Yu-jui Peng and Jui-i Huang, mistroom specialises in projects in the performing arts sector, book binding, and packaging design.

MIUNA
Pages 136-137

MIUNA is brand strategy agency that supports businesses in generating distinctive experiences for clients through design.

Mona Bianca Dürer
Pages 034-037

A media designer, idea hunter, techno lover, and at-times cheeky collector of banalities, Mona Bianca Dürer is passionate about print and analogue work. As a student at DHBW Ravensburg, she discovered a love for unusual approaches and strong concepts, which she has since applied to creating meaningful work for people with meaningful visions.

Monotypo Studio
Pages 096-097

As a business service agency specialising in visual communication and graphic design, Monotypo Studio aims to leave a graphic impression of simple, clean, yet effective aesthetics and functionality on every project.

okapi studio
Pages 064-065

okapi studio in Hong Kong strives to find a balance between development and cultural heritage. It aims to unleash the potential of simple materials and bring creativity into people's lives by celebrating the uniqueness of materiality and redefining them via product design and craftsmanship.

Overdrive Design
Pages 148-149

Overdrive Design is a multidisciplinary agency that has been kicking brands into overdrive since 1986. Located in downtown Hamilton, it solves brand and communications challenges to positively impact businesses through a strong focus on design thinking and technology.

Paprika
Pages 058-059

Paprika is a graphic design and strategic marketing firm in Montreal that specialises in business communications services. It has won more than 800 national and international awards for design excellence since it opening its doors in 1991.

Patryk Hardziej
Pages 138-139

Polish illustrator, graphic designer, and researcher Patryk Hardziej is the originator and curator of 'The Second Polish Exhibition of Graphic Marks' - an international exhibition of Polish design that has been held in five countries. Besides collaborating with local and international brands and institutions, he is also a lecturer at the Academy of Fine Arts in Gdańsk.

Sagmeister & Walsh
Pages 134-135

Sagmeister & Walsh is a creative agency based in New York City. It is a full-service studio specialising in strategy, design, production work across all platforms, including brand identities, campaigns, social strategy, content creation, commercials, websites, apps, books, and environments.

Servaire & Co
Pages 060-063

Servaire & Co is a Paris-based global art direction agency that was founded in 2000 by Sébastien Servaire, a passionate designer who believes that design-thinking is the cornerstone of all brand experiences. The team work with leading beauty and spirits brands by always adopting a 360° approach to design while never shying away from challenges.

(shame-on-you) office

(shame-on-you) office is an official bureau of multidisciplinary design solutions based in Xiamen. Occupied by London College of Communication graduates, Ray and Rose, who have lived and worked in London, Shanghai, and Taiwan, the duo aims to resolve visual, mental, or physical awkwardness via its design ideologies and methodologies.

Studio Blackburn

Studio Blackburn is a London-based design and brand consultancy that aims to make brilliant work through campaigns fit for the modern world. With an experienced, energetic, talented, and ambitious team that values relationships, it partners with risk-takers and decision-makers to effect a positive difference in the world.

studio inbetween

South Korean-born product designer Kiseung Lee studied design and architecture in Helsinki before founding his Berlin-based studio. He explores ecological and sustainable perspectives in pursuing distinctive and artistic views.

Studio Wete

Joan Ramon Pastor, also known as Wete, is a Spanish graphic designer based in Barcelona. Having painted graffiti since his childhood, he loves letterforms, typography, and the complexity of simple things.

studio yumakano

Yuma Kano graduated from the department of design at Tokyo Zokei University and worked as an assistant to artist Yasuhiro Suzuki before founding studio yumakano in Tokyo. Through his award-winning work, he aims to inspire a fun and creative world where everyone is able to find new possibilities by exploring unnoticed aspects of the everyday.

Tom Dixon

A restless innovator, Tom Dixon has continued to reinvent himself throughout his design career. Since setting up his own eponymous brand in 2002 to reexamine the relationship between product designers and the industry, he has become a widely celebrated global force in interior design with hubs in major cities around the world; specialising in sculptural qualities and engineered materiality.

Txaber Mentxaka

After a career spanning more than 25 years in graphic design, Bilbao-born Txaber Mentxaka turned to graphic experimentation and developed his skills in 3D creation. His fascination with typography has also allowed him to create a series of 3D typographic styles that can be seen in his work.

vegrande®

By forging strong relationships based on mutual trust and understanding, vegrande® designs effective brand solutions featuring innovative designs that balance artistic sensibilities with the media, materials, and handiwork available.

visionplus

visionplus is a creative studio in Hong Kong that focuses on graphic design, editorial design, and production. It believes in the power of collaboration and working together with clients to achieve their goals and visions.

Zone Studio

Founded in 2014 by Camille Sablonière, David Rimokh, and Vincent Chatele, Zone Studio expresses itself through graphic design, photography, illustration, as well as video and music creation in a variety of fields.

ACKNOWLEDGEMENTS

We would like to specially thank all the designers and studios who are featured in this book for their significant contribution towards its compilation. We would also like to express our deepest gratitude to our producers for their invaluable advice and assistance throughout this project, as well as the many professionals in the creative industry who were generous with their insights, feedback, and time. To those whose input was not specifically credited or mentioned here, we truly appreciate your support.

FUTURE EDITIONS

If you wish to participate in viction:ary's future projects and publications, please send your portfolio to:
submit@victionary.com